AF615440

ON ESP

ON ESP

Robert H. Curtis

illustrated by Allen Davis
and
Joan Freed Curtis

Prentice-Hall, Inc. Englewood Cliffs, N.J.

10 9 8 7 6 5 4 3 2 1

Printed in the United States of America • J

Prentice-Hall International, Inc., London
Prentice-Hall of Australia, Pty. Ltd., North Sydney
Prentice-Hall of Canada, Ltd., Toronto
Prentice-Hall of India Private Ltd., New Delhi
Prentice-Hall of Japan, Inc., Tokyo

Library of Congress Cataloging in Publication Data

Curtis, Robert H.
On E. S. P.

SUMMARY: The author defines various types of psychic phenomena and presents evidence which credits and discredits psychic experiences. Includes experiments which test the reader's e.s.p.

1. Extrasensory perception—Juvenile literature.
[1. Extrasensory perception] I. Title.
BF1321.C87 133.8 74-20901
ISBN 0-13-634311-2

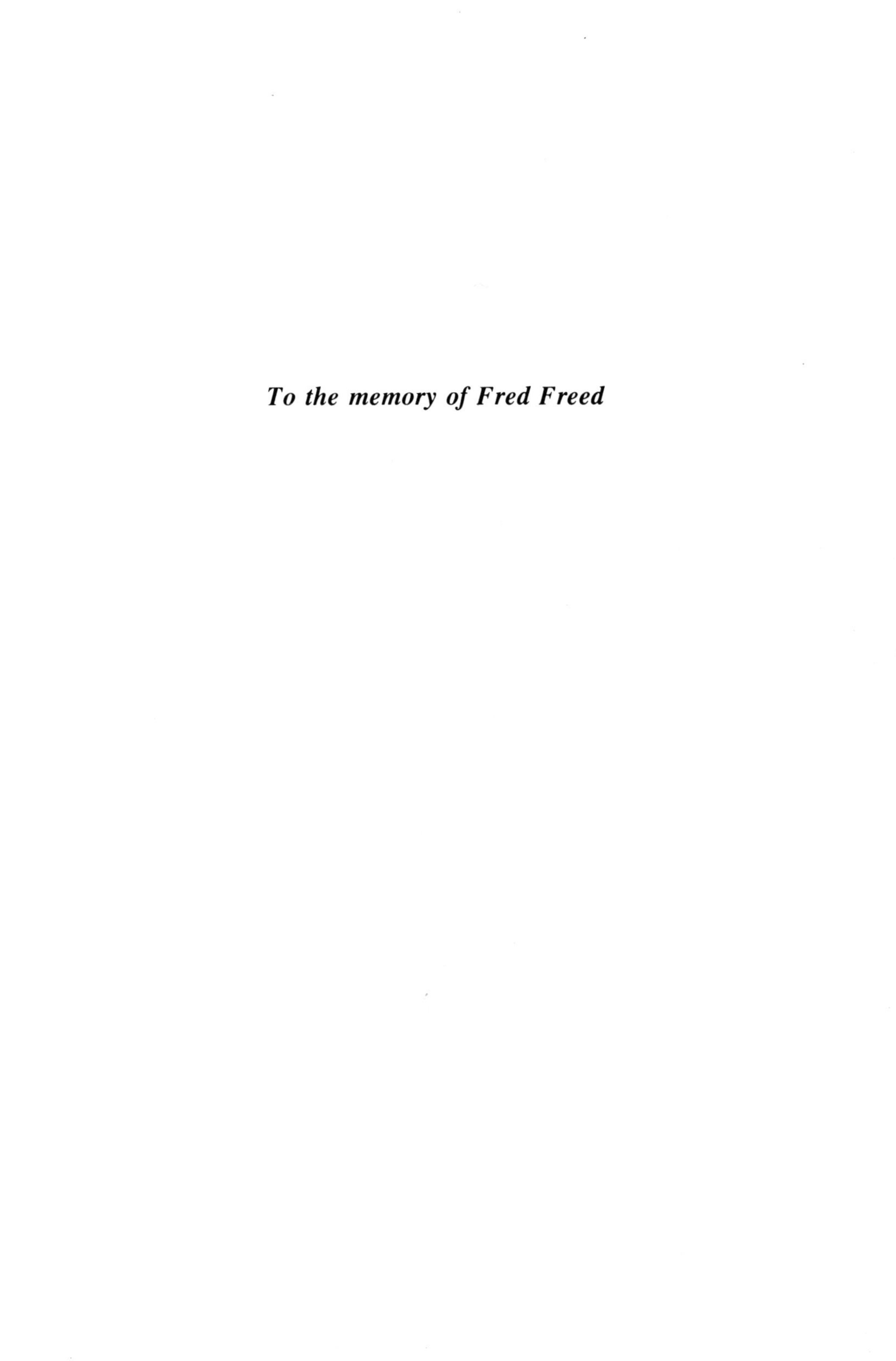

To the memory of Fred Freed

ACKNOWLEDGMENTS

The author thanks the following people for their kindness to him in the preparation of this book: Michelle M. Ackerman; Cedric Clute; Martin Gardner, Editor Mathematical Games Department, *Scientific American;* Professor Ray Hyman, University of Oregon; Professor John A. Jungerman and Professor Charles T. Tart, University of California at Davis; Dr. Stanley Krippner, Maimonides Dream Laboratory; Nadine J. Mortensen; Charles Reynolds, Picture Editor, *Popular Photography;* Dr. Harold Puthoff and Russell Targ, Stanford Research Institute; and Alan Vaughn, Co-editor, Psychic Magazine.

TABLE OF CONTENTS

CHAPTER 1

WHAT IS ESP?

Suppose that a marvelous system of communication existed that very few people were aware of. Let us imagine that, using such a system, we could send and receive messages in a very unusual way. We would be able to let another person know our thoughts without talking or writing. In a similar manner, we would be able to learn somebody else's thoughts without listening to that person or without reading a letter that he or she had written.

Let us further imagine that we would not need any complicated equipment at all and that the messages we send and receive, could travel so powerfully and quickly that, in an instant, they could pass through mountain ranges to get where they were going. This sounds like science fiction, but many important scientists tell us that all this is not fiction but fact—and more than that, we all have the power to use this method of communication. The only equipment we need, they tell us, is our mind.

Today investigators from almost every branch of science are hard at work studying this possible type of mind power called extrasensory perception, or ESP. This special power has been described from the dawn of civilization, but scientists had previously shown little interest in it. What is this phenomenon with which researchers are now so involved? Can we give an example or two of it? Well, a girl thinks about something—say the name of a place—and at that moment happens to open a book and finds the same name she was thinking about right on the page she turned to. "How could that happen?" she asks. Another time, for no particular reason, a boy suddenly gets a strong feeling that something good is going to happen soon, and then a few minutes later it does.

What are the investigators studying these "mysterious" happenings trying to find out? First, they want to learn whether or not these occurrences are more than mere coincidence. Secondly, if they are not simply chance, what is the explanation for them? How do they happen? Can thoughts be sent and received like television programs, by waves sent through the air and received even thousands of miles away?

So far there are more questions in this area than answers, which is exciting in itself. A mystery is always exciting, and scientific mysteries are some of the most stimulating of all. If we have certain thought powers that cannot yet be explained, they deserve careful study. What are the kinds of mental powers many scientists feel we possess, and which are the tests that are going on to learn more about them?

These mental powers are called psychic and the scientists have shortened the word to psi (pronounced sigh). People who have more of these powers than other people are called *psychics*. Soon you will learn how to test yourself and your friends for these special powers. When you do that, you will be a scientist because science is really testing and measuring.

If these special psychic mental powers exist, how do you think they work? Several years ago, a scientist studying this phenomenon used the term extrasensory perception to express his idea of how mental telepathy and other psi powers work. The prefix *extra* means outside of, *sensory* means of or relating to the senses through which we regularly get information, and *perception* means awareness, or receiving the message. Thus ESP means receiving a mental message without the use of the senses we know about. The five most familiar senses are sight, smell, taste, hearing and touch.

Mental messages are thoughts that come from the brain. Although there is a lot of scientific argument about the thinking process, we can regard thoughts as impressions stored in the brain, having been sent there in the first place by the senses. For example, a baby may see several red objects until, finally, it has an idea or thought of "red." Light-wave energy from the various red objects travels through our eyes and continues along optic nerves to the special "seeing" areas of the brain. If these parts of the brain are removed, total blindness results, even if the eyes themselves are perfectly healthy. Therefore, the final step of seeing is actually done by the brain itself. Today, research is being conducted that will enable blind people to see by having pictures sent from a television camera directly to the brain. The camera takes the place of the damaged eyes or optic nerves. In the same way, nerves from the ears, tongue, nose and skin also travel to the brain, bringing messages so that the brain "hears," "tastes," "smells" and "feels" pain and touch, in addition to "seeing."

The memory of "red" might be a simple thought of an infant. When the baby is older, he or she will begin to see apples and after a while the thought "apple" is stored. When the child sees red apples, soon the simple thoughts "red" and "apple" are integrated (put together) into a more complicated thought, "red apple." Later, when the child begins to eat apples, taste impressions give more thoughts about the sweetness of red apples. From these building blocks of thoughts, we accumulate more and more complex ones. Some are original because our imagination gives us the power to put old thoughts together in a new way.

All ESP involves the brain in some way or we would not be thinking or talking or writing about the subject. The result of all our brain activity is what we call the mind, which is a collection of thoughts. *Conscious* thoughts are those we are aware of, but many thoughts are stored in a memory bank called the *subconscious.* "Locked" much of the time, this bank opens for business at night when we are dreaming. People have reported vivid ESP experiences while they were dreaming (we will learn more about the dream world of ESP later).

Throughout history people have always tried to solve riddles about what the future had in store for them. To find the answers, the ancients depended on ESP, although their perceptions were called by other names. The Bible contains many predictions about the future, some of which were made by men called prophets. The ancient Greeks asked the gods for advice about wars, where to establish new towns, or the outcome of their lives. They acted on the advice given them by priestesses who had

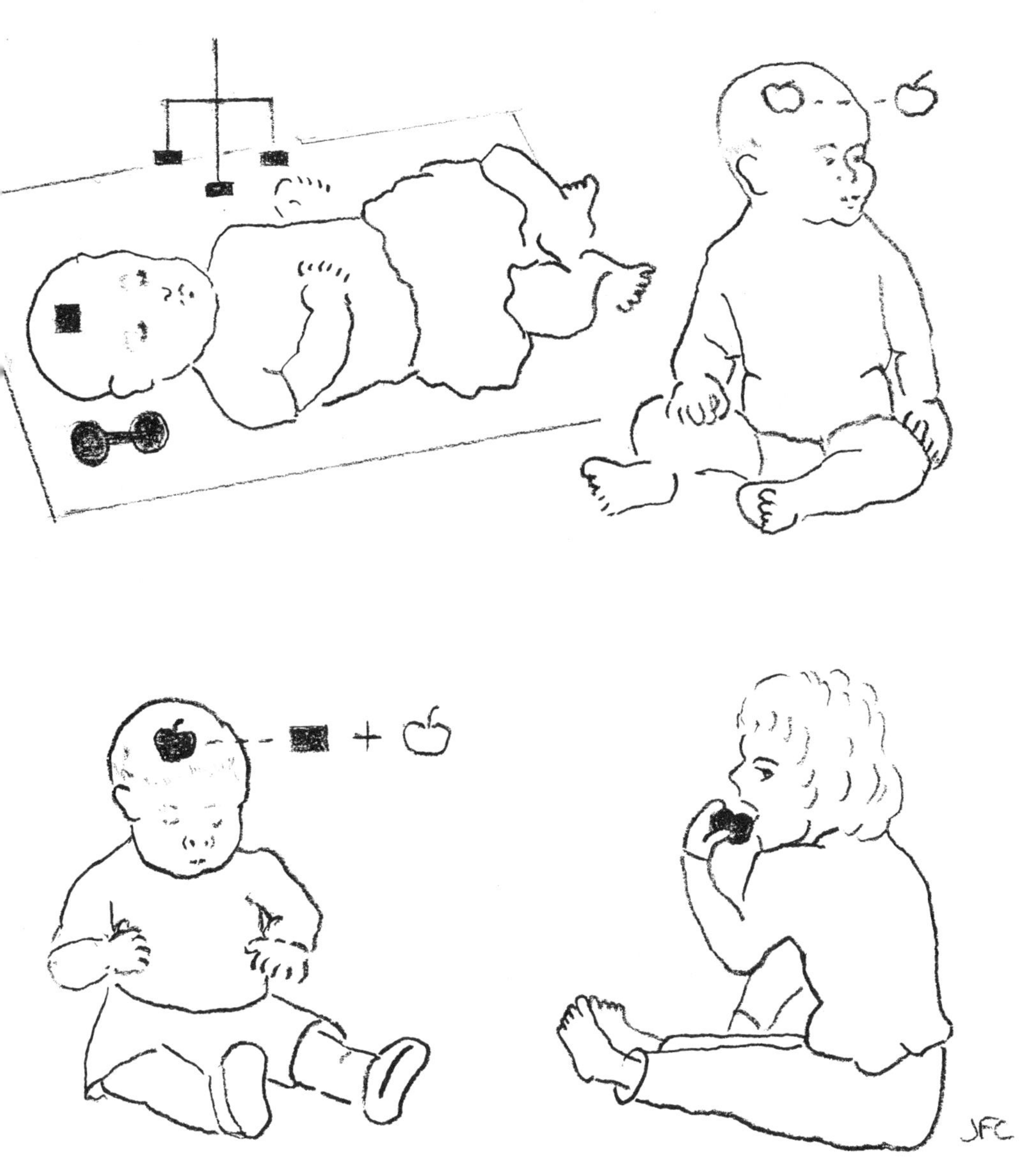
JFC

the "power" to receive information from the gods.

In England in the sixteenth century, William Shakespeare probably believed in ESP, for many characters in his plays make prophecies or have dreams about the future. In addition, we find in Shakespeare, in the Bible and in many other sources strong interest in forms of ESP other than prophecy. These reports tell of visions and mind reading, as well as communications with the ghosts of dead people who live in the spirit world.

By 1882, belief in the spirit world had become so widespread that a group of English scientists formed the Society for Psychical Research. These men felt that scientific study in the field of psychic experiences had been neglected while other sciences, such as chemistry and physics, had received much attention. Reports made by the society stirred up a great deal of excitement, which led a few years later to the formation of similar groups in the United States and other parts of the world. However, it wasn't until the 1930s, when an American psychologist, Dr. J. B. Rhine, founded the first parapsychology laboratory at Duke University, that measurement studies became widely known. This science that deals with the investigation of psychic phenomena and abilities is called *parapsychology*. Today studies are being conducted at universities all over the world. In the United States alone over one hundred colleges offer courses in parapsychology.

CHAPTER 2
MENTAL TELEPATHY

The doorbell rings. When you open the door you are overjoyed and amazed. Standing there is a friend whom you haven't seen for a year but have been thinking about during the past half hour. Was your thinking about your friend responsible for the visit? Did your thought waves reach your friend?

A boy, while riding his bike along with a friend, suddenly gets a very strong feeling that something is wrong with his sister, who is home alone. He seems to hear her call out, tells his friend that he has to leave and races home. As he enters the house, he hears her crying out his name. He runs down the basement stairs and finds his sister lying on the floor. She has fallen down the stairs and is unable to move. Did this boy receive a mental message from his sister?

Many people believe that such episodes are not due to chance at all, that strong feelings can be communicated in a special way. They don't know exactly how this process called *telepathy* works, but they feel sure that thoughts can be sent by one person and received by another.

Does distance make any difference? Psi investigators say no. They believe that an astronaut, while still on the moon, was successful in sending mental messages to earth and that it's just as easy to send a thought from California and have it received in New York as it is from one room to another in the same house.

Are there such things as "waves" of thought energy traveling through the air, and are they like other kinds of energy? Most psi investigators have no physical explanation for the way mental messages travel. But such messages supposedly travel any distance and even through large mountain ranges. No form of energy known to modern science can do that.

Generally people working in the field of telepathy agree that the closer the relationship and understanding between two people, the better the chance for mental messages to travel from one to the other. The most favorable telepathy team is thought to be mother and child. When you begin testing and performing experiments, you may do better with a close friend as a partner than with someone you don't especially like.

CHANCE

Some events happen because of a definite cause; others happen by luck or, as scientists say, by chance. To prove that ESP exists, investigators must show by their tests that the results are due to psi ability and not to lucky guesses.

You can demonstrate how chance works by doing a simple experiment. Get four objects exactly alike except for color. Select the colors red, yellow, blue and green. You can use crayons, marking pens, blocks or balls. Put the four objects in a large pan, blindfold yourself, and shake the pan around to mix the objects. Then reach for one without trying to pick a particular color. Take off your blindfold, look at the object and replace it. You'll be able to get the red object on an average of once every four times. In other words, you have a one-in-four chance of picking it since there are four equal choices. You might have to try forty or fifty times to get a good average, because lucky streaks also occur by chance and you might get the red object three times in a row. However, if you keep trying, your average should be one in four. Now remove the green object, leaving only the red, blue and yellow ones in the pan. Again do the blindfold experiment. Shake the pan each time before picking up the object, remove the blindfold and look at the object. This time, because there are only three choices, by chance you will be successful one out of three times. If you remove the yellow object, leaving only the red and blue, you should be able to pick the red object about half the time because there are only two possibilities. A coin toss works the same way; there are only two possibilities—heads or tails. Now that you've done your first experiment, you know what chance is.

PLAYING-CARD TELEPATHY

Begin your ESP laboratory by getting a new deck of cards. Remove the jokers so that the deck contains 52 cards. Have a friend shuffle the deck and place it face down. Sit across from your partner so that you cannot see the card faces. Have your friend pick one card from the deck, look at it and concentrate on its color. Then try some mind reading and call out the color of the card your friend is looking at. After each answer, have your partner put the card aside, not telling you whether you are right or wrong but keeping score until you've gone through the entire deck. Since there are an equal number of red and black cards in the deck, by chance you should get close to half the correct answers, about 26. On some runs you may score high, perhaps 30 correct guesses; on others you may score low, perhaps 22. But if you keep playing, eventually your average *without trying* will be close to 26 correct answers. If your average is consistently higher and you get many more correct than incorrect guesses when you *concentrate,* experimenters would consider you to be a "sensitive" subject with ESP abilities. As you do the experiment, make sure that your partner doesn't hold up the card too close to a bright light, because you may be able to see rather than sense its color. (If you hold a card up to a bright light, you'll be able to see through the back and identify the card.)

Now reverse the procedure. You concentrate on the card and let your friend try to read your mind as you keep score. Scientists call the person who is looking at the card and concentrating on it the "agent" while the person who is doing the mind reading is called the "percipient." However, we will use the simpler words, "sender" and "receiver."

You can make the experiment more difficult if you try to guess the exact suit—clubs, diamonds, hearts or spades. Since there are 13 cards of each suit in a deck of 52 cards, the chance of a correct guess is one out of four. If, after going through the entire deck several times, and in each run you guessed the correct suit 14 or more times, your record would be above chance. Investigators feel that the higher the number of correct guesses by the receiver, the more the ESP ability. They also feel that consistently low scores (below chance) are due to ESP but they are caused by a negative psi effect.

Now make your experiment even harder. Take the ace through the ten of hearts (counting the ace as 1). Have your friend shuffle the cards and you try to guess the exact card as he looks at it and concentrates on it. You can keep your eyes either closed or open, but if you keep them open, make sure you don't see the face of the card or get any hint of its identity from the back of it. If you feel that a card is the same one you mentioned a few tries ago, it doesn't matter. You can repeat. By chance, you should get one correct answer from the ten cards. If you do better consistently, you have exceeded the law of averages.

To do the most difficult card test of all, try to guess the exact card that your friend is looking at and concentrating on; for example, the 9 of clubs or the queen of hearts. Your chances of getting a correct answer are very small—1 out of 52. Can you beat the odds?

As you do your experiments keep a record of your scores.

ZENER-CARD TELEPATHY

The first research in telepathy in an American university was performed by John E. Coover, a psychology professor at Stanford University. After 10,000 card-guessing tests similar to the ones you just did, no evidence for the existence of mental telepathy was found and the work was discontinued.

Then some years later, in 1934, Dr. Rhine published a book *Extra-Sensory Perception* in which he claimed that his experiments had shown without doubt that ESP existed and that it could be tested in the laboratory.

A colleague of Dr. Rhine's, K.E. Zener, designed a set of cards, which became the standard test cards for various ESP experiments.

As you can see, Zener drew five different designs—a plus sign, a star, a circle, some wavy lines and a square. There are five cards of each design, making a total of twenty-five cards in the deck. You can easily add to your home ESP laboratory by making a set of Zener cards. You can use index cards or make cards from cardboard. If you use cardboard cutouts, be sure the sides and back of the cards are identical so no clue will be obtained from the appearance of the card itself. Use a marking pen or crayon to draw the designs, making sure that you don't press too hard so that an impression is made on the back of the card. Remembering the rules of chance, you can see that since there are five symbols, you have a one-in-five chance of getting the right card with any guess and close to five correct answers when a run of the entire deck is made.

Now perform the experiment with this deck in the same way that you did with your ordinary deck of playing cards. Have your friend hold up each card in turn, showing only the back of it to you. Take as long as you like, and when you are ready, call out the symbol—star, wavy line, plus sign, square or circle—depending on what you visualize in your mind. Don't try to remember what you've already said. For example, in one run, you might guess "star" ten times even though you know that there are only five star cards in the deck. You have to treat each card as if you are starting all over again. Have your friend keep a score card with the symbol of the correct card on one side and your guess on the other; then total the number of your correct answers. The most successful of Dr. Rhine's subjects, a divinity student at Duke, averaged eight hits per run after looking at 17,250 cards. Any average above five over a long period of time would be a good result.

CRAIG SINCLAIR EXPERIMENTS

About forty-five years ago, a famous writer named Upton Sinclair participated with his wife in a fascinating series of telepathy experiments. Sinclair was a social reformer whose reputation was so great that he had nothing to gain and everything to lose when he published a book about these unusual experiments.

Mr. Sinclair made a drawing in one room while his wife Craig was in another room. She composed herself into a relaxed state by turning down the light and thinking for a while about something pleasant, like a flower. When her mind was completely relaxed, she told her husband to begin. He then drew a picture, after which she closed her eyes and tried to visualize it. Sometimes the picture "came" in fragments and she waited until it was complete. The outline of the picture appeared in dark gray lines, which showed up over the light gray background formed when her eyes were closed. When she received the picture, she drew it on a piece of paper and said "Ready." Her husband then came in from the other room and they compared the two pictures. They scored her results as successes, partial successes, and failures, and in 290 experiments there was success or partial success in over three quarters of them. Below are a series of their drawings. The ones on the left were drawn by Upton Sinclair; those on the right were drawn by Craig Sinclair after she had visualized the picture in her mind and before she had actually seen her husband's drawings.

You can do this experiment with one person or several. If a group is participating, one person should do the original drawing and the others should be in separate locations trying to reproduce it. Comparisons should be made with the original drawing only when all the participants are ready.

It is interesting to know how Mrs. Sinclair trained herself to do these drawings. She was a very honest woman who despised fraud, and she felt that the only way she could convince herself

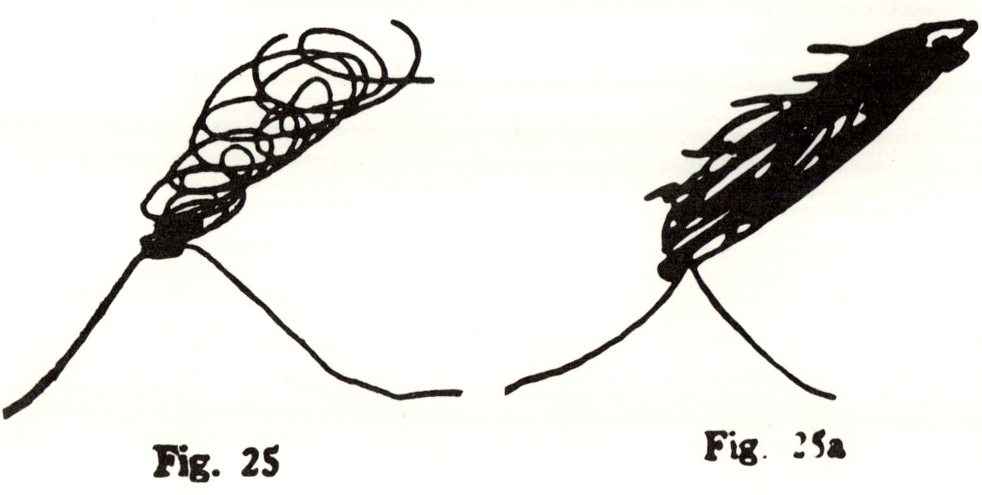

Fig. 25

Fig. 25a

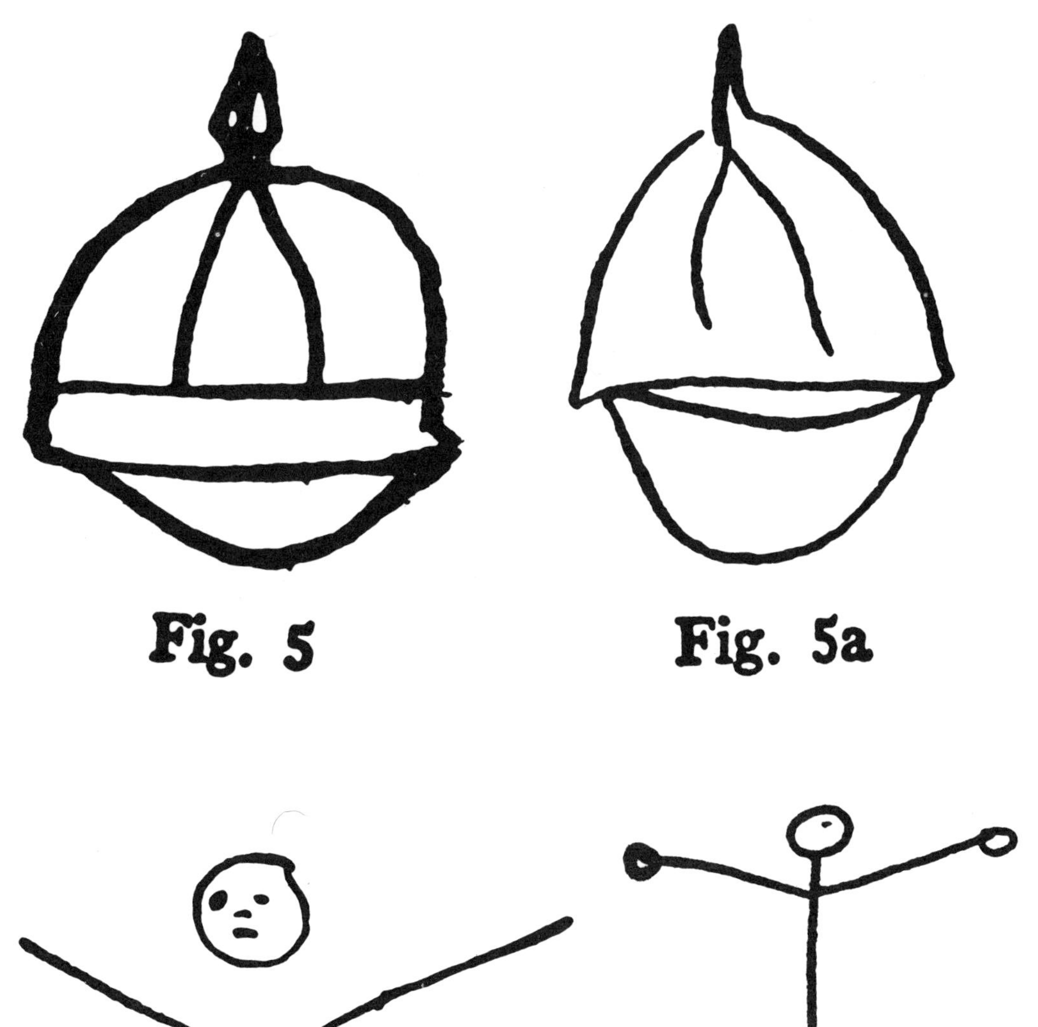

Fig. 5 **Fig. 5a**

Fig. 9

May be elephant's mouth — but any way it is some kind of a running animal

Fig. 9a

that telepathy existed was to experiment and not take the word of others. She would have somebody draw about six simple designs—triangles, squares, circles, etc.—on cards and fold them. After lying down and relaxing until her mind was a complete blank, she would reach for the top drawing from the pile, which she had placed on a table close by. Holding the card in her hand, she would place it on her stomach, keeping her eyes closed, and say with her mind, "I want to see what is on this card." After practice, she became very successful and then began the experiments with her husband in the other room. Learning this technique may take a while, but the experiment should prove to be very exciting.

You now have a good start on your ESP lab. Remember that investigators who believe in ESP claim that distance is no barrier. Have fun by trying some of these card-guessing and drawing experiments over the telephone with friends.

CHAPTER 3

CLAIRVOYANCE AND PRECOGNITION

Clairvoyance is knowledge obtained about an object or an event without the use of the senses. The word comes from two French words meaning "clear seeing" and is sometimes called *second sight.*

If a girl is standing alone at the ocean shore and sees a ship sinking, she may be the only one who knows what is happening aside from those on the ship or those notified by the ship's radio. Since she is getting her information from sight, one of the senses, she would not be clairvoyant. On the other hand, suppose that she dreams of a ship hitting an iceberg, and in her dream she sees the name of the ship and is so frightened that she wakes up and looks at the time. It is 2:30 a.m. The next evening, she reads that a ship bearing the same name as the one in her dream sank at approximately the time of her dream. That would be a possible clairvoyant experience because seemingly she could have obtained this knowledge only by ESP. Are there other possible explanations? Suppose a neighbor had his radio on and the girl heard a news bulletin of the sinking while asleep?

Clairvoyance also is tested in the laboratory, but unlike telepathy, an agent is not required. The experimental subject is both sender and receiver. For example, he looks at a card which is face down so he can't tell what it is. Then, by clairvoyance he tries to "see" the name of the card with his mind.

Among several varieties of clairvoyance, one is *precognition* in which the person is able to "see" events that will occur in the future. Suppose that the girl dreamed about the sinking ship *a week before it actually sank.* If she remembers her vivid dream the next morning and immediately tells someone the details—the name of the ship, the iceberg, the collision and sinking—this would undoubtedly be a true case of precognition. Knowledge of all these details, including the time of the sinking, a week before the tragedy, would certainly not be due to coincidence.

Another type of clairvoyance is called *retrocognition*, in which someone may describe a place never visited or begin to speak a language never learned. There have been such cases reported by investigators who believe in reincarnation, rebirth of a soul in a new body many years or even centuries later. In India, a boy claimed to be the reincarnation of a man who had died. It was reported in 1966 that the boy was taken to the town where he had "died" in 1951. He spoke to the widow, who tested him by asking many questions, the answers to which only she and her former husband knew. The boy answered the questions in amazing detail and even traveled with the widow to a nearby town, where he recognized other members of the family and seemed completely familiar with the house in which they lived. It should be remembered that hearsay evidence tends to become exaggerated at best and may be completely fraudulent at worst. Are there explanations for retrocognition such as stored memories of other people's conversations or some sort of hypnosis?

CLAIRVOYANCE EXPERIMENTS

Gather five completely different objects such as a coin, a key, a pencil, a ring and a comb. Any objects will do so long as they are different, and you may use more than five if you wish. Bring the objects on a small tray into a room where you've gathered a group of friends. Have everybody study the objects to become familiar with them. Then select a person to take the tray into another room, place one of the objects in the center of that room and put aside the tray with the remaining four objects. Then have the person return to the group and let everybody concentrate to visualize the object that was placed in the center of the other room. When each of you feels you know the answer, write it on a piece of paper with your name and place the paper face down on a table. When everyone is finished, go into the next room and see who got the correct answer.

You can change this experiment a bit by having the person place all five objects in a row in the other room and then have the group try to guess their order.

Instead of objects you can use five pictures of well-known people cut out of newspapers or magazines, or pictures on baseball cards or even snapshots of friends or family members. If you are by yourself, place each photograph in an opaque envelope and shuffle them so that you don't know the location of the pictures. Place the envelopes in line on the floor and concentrate on each one in turn. When you think you know whose picture is in each envelope, write down the names. Then open the envelopes and keep your score. With practice, you will be able to improve. Check to see if you got better results with the photographs than you did with the objects. Many investigators feel there's more psi ability with photographs of people than with objects. What do you find?

The card experiments described in the telepathy chapter, using both an ordinary deck of playing cards as well as a Zener deck, can be changed slightly for clairvoyance experiments. If the immediate, or "now," type of clairvoyance is being tested, simply write down your answers as you get impressions from the backs of the cards you have shuffled. No one else has to look at the cards, since you are testing clairvoyance and not telepathy.

Psi investigators say that by holding and touching an object belonging to a person, much information about the character of that person can be obtained. Have a friend bring some small personal objects belonging to members of his family, without revealing the identity of the owners. Take one object at a time and hold it. If you get any feelings, any vibrations, about the object's owner, tell your friend. Then find out if you came close in any of your comments. This type of psi ability is called *psychometry.*

To test for *precognitive clairvoyance,* for what will happen in the future, you can again use the card and the five-object experiments. In doing the card experiments with the Zener deck, for example, write a list of the twenty-five cards in the order in which you think they will turn up. Then shuffle the deck and look at the cards, one by one. How good was your predictive ability?

With the five objects, make a list of the order in which you think your friend will set down the objects. Then have your partner take the objects into the next room and set them down in a line. The reason for using the other room is to avoid any accidental influence by sound or gesture as the objects are put in place. Again you will be able to see how well you did.

It should be challenging and fun to invent new experiments yourself and add to your ESP laboratory. See if you can devise some new tests.

Clairvoyance experiences are among the most interesting in the psi literature because they are usually so dramatic. Often a warning heard in a dream results in a life saved. A girl had a nightmare in which her mother frantically called out to her. The girl awoke, frightened, and got out of bed. Just as she reached her dressing table, a roof beam suddenly fell, crushing the bed. The next day, her mother, who was visiting a relative hundreds of miles away, telephoned to tell her that she had a terrible dream in which she saw her daughter in great danger. Coincidence? The girl will never believe that. Would you?

When someone with supposed psychic powers tells what is going to happen in the future, the event he or she forecasts is seldom unimportant. It would seem silly to say: "I predict that in two years the Peabody School gym floor will be revarnished." However, when that same psychic makes the pronouncement, "I predict that in two years the entire state of Florida will suddenly disappear under the Atlantic Ocean, never to rise again," people reading the prediction become attentive, especially if they happen to live in Florida.

For a number of reasons it is very difficult to tell if someone really possesses psychic powers. Can you think of some of the reasons? Often the predictions are so general they are very likely to come true. For example, if a psychic predicts that in a year or so there will be a big scandal in Washington, D.C., that prediction will probably come true because there is *always* some kind of government scandal being discovered. Then again, nobody is sure how many predictions a psychic is making. The only ones we hear about are those that come true, because the failures are never mentioned. Recently, one of America's most famous psychics made a number of predictions at the beginning of the year about what would happen during the coming year. These forecasts were made on a national television show. At the end of the year, the tape of the program was replayed and not one of the predictions made was correct.

Some psychics are more modest than their fellow prophets. Alan Vaughan is a well-educated and intelligent man who is coeditor of *Psychic Magazine.* He feels that psychic powers are not a special gift, given to a certain chosen few. Rather, he believes that every person has psi powers and, furthermore, that a person can learn to improve his ability with study. Many ESP investigators agree with him.

Alan Vaughan did something unusual for most psychics. He was so disturbed about two dreams concerning the assassination of Robert F. Kennedy that he acted on these premonitions, or early warnings. He was studying in Europe at the time and feels these dreams were triggered by the assassination of Martin Luther King, Jr. He kept a dream diary and recorded: ". . . it was dark . . . the killer . . . hid . . . to fire one shot from a rifle to murder the person; he thought of firing more shots; he was a person people did not suspect. A party is planned; many people come, including Senator Kennedy . . . I got into a central hall connecting all the rooms . . . In the first room is a group of young people. Kennedy must be in the other room, I think . . ." Vaughan immediately sent letters describing these dreams to the Society of Psychical Research in London and to the Maimonides Dream

Laboratory in Brooklyn. He sent his letters on May 25, 1968, giving his strong feelings that Senator Kennedy would be shot soon. Kennedy was assassinated on June 5, 1968, in the kitchen hallway of the Ambassador Hotel in Los Angeles.

Vaughan feels that about one out of ten dreams is a precognitive one and that much research should be done in this field so that tragedies might possibly be prevented. To this end, there are now premonition registries to which people can report their feelings about future events well before these events are supposed to happen. In this way it may also be possible to find out if any person can be fairly consistent in correctly predicting the future.

Occasionally, people in authority feel strongly enough about their dreams to act on them. Recently, an administrator of Alameda Hospital in California had a vivid dream about an air crash and ordered the hospital to prepare additional emergency plans and services. Soon afterward, a Navy jet crashed into an apartment house in Alameda, causing many casualties. When these victims were brought to the hospital, the preparatory measures were lifesaving.

Frequently people who claim special clairvoyant and other poorly-understood powers are challenged by others who don't believe such powers exist. For instance, Dr. Abraham Kovoor, of Sri Lanka (formerly Ceylon), has deposited a currency note in a safety deposit box. He has offered $16,500 to anyone who can tell the serial number of this note. That's a pretty good incentive to demonstrate clairvoyant powers, but Dr. Kovoor still has his money. He has also shown that there is nothing mysterious about walking on hot coals; the walker's feet are protected by a thin layer of ash as he dashes across the coals. His demonstration infuriated those who believed that this activity required mystical powers. He has also lived in "haunted" houses to disprove the existence of ghosts.

Dr. Kovoor hasn't convinced everybody that ghosts don't exist. One of these people is a London housewife named Mrs. Rosemary Brown. She regularly receives visits from dead composers who give her their latest musical creations. Liszt, Chopin, Schubert, Beethoven and others have been very generous with her, visiting frequently, and showing that they are still hard at work. When she talks with Grieg, who reminds her of a "great big shaggy dog," she would appear to have an out-of-this-world type of clairvoyance—an astral clairvoyance. If the existence of this power is proved in the laboratory, Mrs. Brown's visitors won't seem as far out as they do today.

You can now make some additions to your ESP laboratory. Begin a Premonitions Notebook. If you get a very strong feeling about something important which you believe will happen in the future, or you have a dream about such an event, write the details in your notebook. You can also send the information to the Central Premonitions Registry, Box 482, Times Square Station, New York, N.Y. 10036, or to Premonitions Registry Bureau, Mind's Ear, KPFA Radio, Berkeley, California 94704. In addition, keep a scrapbook of various psychics' predictions that are reported in newspapers or on television from time to time. Follow up to check if these predictions prove to be accurate or not.

DATE OF PREMONITION	PREMONITION	WHAT ACTUALLY HAPPENED	DATE IT HAPPENED
1/17/75	thinking about	Received a letter	1/27/75
	Mary Jane	from Mary Jane	
4/20/75	thought I'd win	Won 3rd place	4/21/75
	1st place in the		
	Spelling test		

CHAPTER 4

PSYCHOKINESIS

Approximately a half century ago magician showmanship reached the height of its popularity. Names like Houdini, Thurston, Carter and Blackstone were known all over the world, and when these men gave performances in large theaters or auditoriums the house was usually "sold out." These shows created the same kind of excitement in their day as the Super Bowl does now. The magicians used large expensive equipment for their tricks, which were called illusions. For example, a magician doesn't really saw a woman assistant in half—he just *appears* to be doing so. If he really sawed the woman in half, he would hardly be using the same assistant show after show. And besides, he wouldn't have many volunteers for the job.

One of the favorite illusion acts of the famous magicians was the act of levitation, the appearance of raising a body from a table in seeming defiance of gravity by using "mind power," supposedly demonstrating that the mind could influence material objects like a human body. Today, many scientists feel that mind over matter can be more than illusion and may represent a real psi power. Although *psychokinesis*, or PK as it is called, is included within ESP, actually it is slightly different. Can you see why? In PK, the perception element of ESP is absent. In telepathy and clairvoyance, the mental message comes *in* to the person who receives it. In PK, the mental message goes *out* to the object with the idea of making it respond in the desired way. Still, it involves a mental message and scientists who believe that ESP exists feel that PK is a manifestation of the psi process.

PK did not attract the attention that its psi relatives, telepathy and clairvoyance, did until a few years ago when a young Israeli, Uri Geller, became world known for his dramatic exhibition of unusual mental abilities. The most spectacular of these was his apparent ability to bend and sometimes break hard metal objects after gently stroking them for a brief period of time. He would mentally "order" objects such as keys, spoons, and the like to bend.

Born December 20, 1946, Geller became aware of his telepathic powers at an early age when he could identify the cards his mother was holding when they played games. He claims that at the age of three he had a mystical experience and saw a flying saucer while playing in the garden of an estate in Jaffa. While in school, he discovered that by concentrating he could move the hands of his watch backward or forward, and soon he was showing this "trick" to schoolmates.

When he grew up, a friend convinced him to use his telepathic and PK powers in a stage act. His performances were very popular and eventually he was induced by an American doctor to come to the United States. Geller agreed to be the subject of a scientific investigation at the Stanford Research Institute, a renowned private laboratory once affiliated with Stanford University. Geller was studied at the institute for several months,during which time he demonstrated every type of psi ability. The experiments were filmed by an expert, and every effort was made to make sure that no cheating could take place. The film is remarkable, and if no trickery was involved in Geller's demonstrations, the results would represent a fantastic breakthrough in proving the existence of ESP. However, several magicians have stated that they could duplicate everything that Geller did at S.R.I. The controversy rages on, complicated by the fact that Geller has been caught cheating during many demonstrations where magicians trained to observe deception have been present. Uri's believers have excused any deception on the basis that he is a showman after all, and when his psi powers fail him, it is natural for him to use magicians' tricks to make sure his show is a good one. At the present time Uri Geller claims that all his powers come from an intelligence from outer space called "Hoova." Again, we don't know if this is show business or not.

PSYCHOKINESIS EXPERIMENTS

You can try several PK experiments. First, add a series of coins to your ESP laboratory—a penny, nickel, dime, quarter and half dollar. You and your friends will be flipping these coins and some may prefer the half dollar while others may find the smallest, the dime, easiest to flip. Flip a coin and while it is in midair, "tell" the coin to land either heads or tails. Again, record your hits and misses. As with the red and black cards, your chance of success on each flip is one out of two; by chance the coin will land the way you want it to half the time. If you can somehow "influence" the movement of the coin so that it lands the way you wish more frequently than average over a long period of time, this could be considered evidence of PK ability.

Next, get a die (one of a pair of dice) and throw it against a wall trying to get a certain number to land face up. Since the die has six faces, each bearing a different number of dots, your chance rate of success will be one out of six. In thirty-six tries for a four, if the number lands face up seven or more times, you would be doing better than chance. However, you would have to come up with *four* over a long period of time with many trials for the result to be what mathematicians call "statistically significant." That means that the likelihood of your good result was due to luck is very small.

For centuries people known as dowsers have been employed to find the presence of underground water or minerals. Somebody wanting to know where on his property he could dig a well might hire a dowser. Holding a wooden stick or metal rod, the dowser walks around the area until the stick suddenly dips down toward the ground, indicating a place where water is present. These sticks were called divining rods, and it was thought that supernatural or magical powers were involved. The latest interpretation is that ESP is involved, and when the dowser "feels" the presence of water, his hand will automatically move and the stick will dip downward at the right spot. Traditionally, forked wooden sticks are used. You can pick up a small forked stick (about five or six inches long) in a park or in the country.

Now you and your friends can try an experiment. Get three

JFC

or four pots, with lids, each large enough to hold a glass of water. Send one of the group, the dowser, out of the room; then place a glass of water in one of the pots and put the lids on all the pots. Call the dowser back into the room, hand him or her the divining rod and ask the subject to find the pot with the glass of water. See if the stick will suddenly dip downward when it is held over the correct pot. Make sure nobody gives any hints to the dowser. Hints, or what scientists call "sensory cues," are often communicated so that the subject gets the correct answer from the reactions of the observers or through sounds rather than an ESP channel.

You might want to try an experiment that combines telepathy and psychokinesis. Place two identical glasses filled with a beverage side by side on a table. Ask one person to leave the room; the rest of the group then decides which glass they want the subject to drink from, the one on the right or the one on the left. Have the subject return to the room and stand facing the two glasses. Now everybody must concentrate hard on the selected glass. When everybody has nodded, indicating that concentration is going on, one person tells the subject to go ahead and drink. Again, by chance, the answer will be correct half the time. Let each subject have six or so consecutive tries. He or she should drink only a sip each time, or your supply of milk or soft drinks may run out fairly soon. Maybe the best idea is to use water.

Finally, you may want to experiment to see if thoughts can influence plant growth. Many people have claimed that plants respond to human emotions and that prayer and love can greatly benefit a plant's health and development. Purchase a packet of flower or vegetable seeds, divide them in half, and plant each group in a separate container. Think good thoughts about one group, wishing these seeds well in their journey to planthood.

You can think mean thoughts about the other group if you want, but it is important that you not talk to the plants. However, if you do, talk an equal amount of time to each group because the carbon dioxide from your lungs will in itself be an aid to growth. You can make the experiment even more scientific by having someone else in the house take care of the plants, doing the watering, feeding, etc. Don't tell that person which of the two containers, A or B, you're rooting for. It will be interesting to see if the seeds that you want to flourish produce much healthier plants than those in the other container.

The experiments just described are all rather crude but they are actual PK experiments and the only type performed until recently. Of course, some scientific gadgets have been used, such as automatic coin tossers and automatic dice throwers, to further eliminate chance of human error, but none of these approaches the scientific precision of a PK experiment being conducted by a nuclear physicist at the University of California at Davis. Professor John A. Jungerman has invented a testing device so sensitive that the impact of molecules of light can be measured (light can exert pressure). This machine uses a laser beam of light, which shines on a mirror. The subject sits in a chair and tries concentrating to make the mirror move. The most minute movement of the mirror will affect the light, and the movement can be measured. Dr. Jungerman's experiment should provide information as to whether PK exists or not and, further, if it exists, how much force can be exerted by the most gifted subjects.

CHAPTER 5

TRAVELS IN DREAMS

The strongest psi effects can be demonstrated during the dream state, according to investigators working in the ESP field. This is because while we are dreaming our conscious minds are not operating and so the process of stopping certain unpleasant thoughts is turned off. Two types of ESP experiences have been studied during the dream state. In the first of these, an out-of-body experience, or OOBE, only the dreamer himself is involved. In the second, an agent tries to send messages to the dreamer (research in this area is being carried on by the Maimonides Dream Laboratory at Maimonides Hospital in New York).

Dr. Charles T. Tart, professor of Psychology at University of California at Davis, has studied two people who claim the ability to "leave" their sleeping bodies and have their spiritual selves take a trip. Some subjects claiming this power have insisted that they were able to travel hundreds of miles while asleep, returning to their bodies in time to wake up, a process sometimes called *astral projection*. People who have had these experiences feel that they are floating, claim to see their physical bodies from the outside and are absolutely convinced that the experience was not a dream.

The first of the two subjects studied by Dr. Tart was a man whom he called Mr. X. Dr. Tart studied Mr. X for nine sessions, and on the next to last one Mr. X reported an OOBE. Attached to various pieces of equipment to measure brain waves and so forth, the subject slept in one room while Dr. Tart or his technician observed him through a window in another room. At the time during which Mr. X claimed to have had an OOBE, he was able to describe the physical appearance of the technician's husband whom he had never met but who was in the building. In the second case, a woman, Miss Z, was studied in a similar fashion during four evenings. On the last evening, she claimed to have an OOBE and was able to read a target number, 25132, which had been placed face up on a shelf. This number could not have been normally seen from the bed. It would be almost impossible to guess a five-digit number in correct order. However, in both the case of Mr. X and of Miss Z, cheating could not be excluded because, unfortunately, in each instance, there were periods during which the experimenters did not directly observe the subjects. However, Dr. Tart feels that it is important to study people who claim to have this ability and to measure their physiological responses during the time they claim to be out of their bodies.

In the second kind of investigation, being done at Maimonides, while the subject sleeps, he or she is constantly monitored. An observer can tell when the subject is dreaming by watching the eyes. A dreamer's eyes move back and forth very quickly. These movements, called rapid eye movements, or REM, can be detected electrically by eyelid attachments. (You can often see REM in a cat who is enjoying a relaxed nap.) When a subject shows REM sleep, an agent in another room concentrates on a photograph of a painting and tries to "send" the picture he or she is looking at into the mind of the dreamer. When REM sleep is over, the subject is awakened and asked to report the details of the dream. Frequently the investigators have found that the dreamer describes quite accurately the photograph that the agent had attempted to send, a form of mental telepathy.

Similar experiments have been done at Maimonides with subjects who are awake but completely free from any distractions, a state called *sensory deprivation* by the scientists. Here the subject has opaque discs placed over the eyes so that no light can enter, earphones placed over the ears to prevent any sounds from being heard and in general is prepared so that practically no sensory stimulation reaches him. As occurs in the dream state, a subject who is deprived of sensory distractions will be much more receptive to telepathy. After the subject has been prepared and a period of time has passed, the agent tries to send information. In these experiments, the agent looks through a View Master, and generally one of four sets of scenic photographs is randomly selected and viewed by the agent. When the agent begins to look at the series of pictures selected, the subject is told to describe what he or she sees, and the comments are recorded. After each experiment the subject is brought into the room where the agent has been looking at the photographs and is asked to view the four sets and select the one which most closely corresponds to the mental pictures previously seen. The chance of correct selection is one out of four, but after many trials the investigators feel that their success is far better than would be expected by chance. In some instances the comments made by the subjects have been amazingly accurate.

In one instance, the view strip selected was of Las Vegas, Nevada. The first scene was an aerial view and as the agent was concentrating on it, the subject, a girl, described sensations of floating over a city. When the agent turned to the next picture showing hotel signs along the Strip, she described seeing a series of theater marquees with many bright lights. After the experiment was over, the subject picked out the Las Vegas photographs with ease. She was astounded at how much they resembled what she had visualized.

One note of caution: dreams and daydreams are usually so rich in content that it is very difficult to tell what part, if any, has really been influenced by something "sent" by an agent.

Be on the lookout for articles that describe modern experiments in ESP. Having done some of your own, you will be able to appreciate them even more.

CHAPTER 6

FAITH HEALING REVIVED

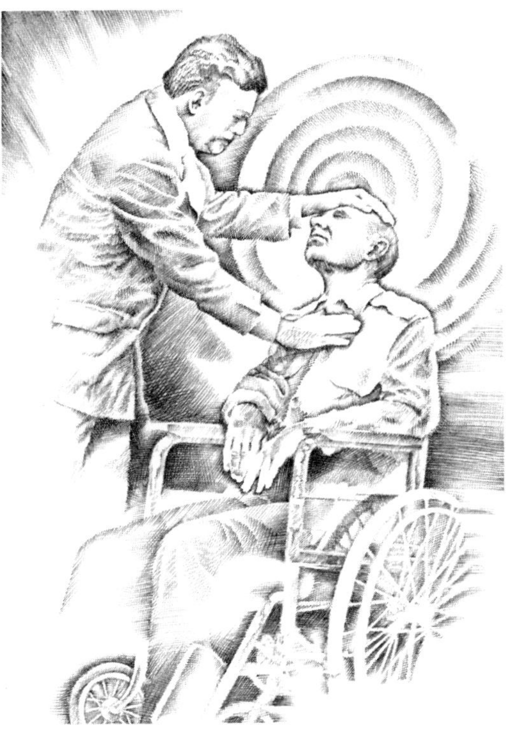

Physicians know that the mind has a powerful influence over the body. In many diseases, the physical signs and symptoms are caused by emotional disturbances. These diseases are called psychosomatic. Stomach ulcers and migraine headaches are almost certainly caused by tension, and tension is probably at least part of the cause of many other diseases, including heart attacks. If tensions are eased, ulcers and headaches disappear, and the likelihood of having a heart attack is lessened. Physicians also recognize that even serious diseases like cancer occasionally go away by themselves, regardless of what the doctor does or doesn't do. The reasons for such apparently miraculous cures are unknown as yet.

It is not hard to see how emotions affect each of us every day of our lives. If we get angry, our faces may get flushed. If we are frightened, we may grow pale and break out in a cold sweat and our hearts may beat much more rapidly. Also we may have to urinate more frequently and school bathrooms are often very busy just before important examinations. If we are embarrassed, we may blush. All of the above effects are caused by changes in the circulation of blood brought about by emotion. Since every organ and system of the body depends on circulation for survival, we can see how widespread the effects of emotion can be. Furthermore, our moods can affect the function of the endocrine glands so important to our health. Thus thyroid disease, diabetes, and other illnesses may be altered by our mental condition. In fact, we do not know today to what extent emotions affect body health. It may well be that every disease known to man may be influenced by emotion. For example, it was discovered years ago at Memorial Hospital in New York City that those patients with cancer who had the "will to live" actually did far better than patients whose disease involvement was the same, but who had given up.

With the increasing investigation of ESP, interest in the medical uses of psychic ability has increased. "Can psychic abilities cure disease?" the parapsychologists have asked. And after much investigation, they have agreed that the answer is yes. The difference between conventional physicians and psychic healers is that physicians believe that many diseases are primarily physical and that diagnosis and cure require the very latest laboratory equipment. Thus treatment may call for extensive surgery under sterile conditions or the use of very complicated drugs; in these instances of serious illness the patient must be closely observed by trained personnel. Many psychic healers, on the other hand, feel that a simple touching procedure accompanied by positive thinking will result in miraculous cures in almost all cases of illness. In fact, in some parts of the world certain healers have claimed the ability to perform psychic surgery. These operations, done by medically untrained people, require no anesthesia and are done without using sterile conditions. The most spectacular claim is that no cutting is involved. For example, a psychic surgeon supposedly places his hand inside a patient's abdomen and pulls out a tumor, all of this without leaving a scar. Psychic surgeons have never operated in the presence of a scientific group so it is impossible to evaluate their claims.

Faith healing is not new. It has existed since the beginning of history, and in primitive societies witch doctors have used similar methods to treat their patients. Not so long ago, the "royal touch" was used by kings who would lightly place their hands on subjects afflicted with diseases. If a subject's leg was paralyzed because of hysteria, which is a disease of the mind rather than of the muscles or nerves of the leg, the "royal touch" was very effective because the patient *believed* that the king had the power to cure him. The "royal touch" ceremony reached its height in the seventeenth century when Charles II was King of England. In those days, treatment sessions were held regularly so that the king could heal those of his subjects who were sick. Sometimes as many as six hundred people came to the palace to be treated. The king would place both his hands on each sick person and give each patient a gold coin called a "touchpiece." After he had completed the touching part of the ritual, he would read from the Bible. Sick people came from all over England for this treatment and the king's reputation was so good that an occasional patient even traveled from America.

Today, faith healing is being studied scientifically in some of the most important medical centers all over the world. In the years to come, we can expect to learn much more about how, why and when faith healing can be used to cure or lessen sickness or even better, as a means of preserving good health.

HYPNOSIS

Since the mind has such a strong influence over all our activities, anything that affects the way we think has tremendous influence on our health. It is not surprising that *hypnosis* is widely used by both physicians and psychic healers. The process is based on suggestion; the patient being hypnotized must have faith that whoever is performing the hypnosis will be successful. The subject has to accept suggestion in order to be hypnotized in the first place, and once hypnotized, he must accept the suggestions of the hypnotist that he get well. How does hypnotism work? Nobody really knows, but the trance state is usually accomplished by concentration of the subject on what the hypnotist is saying; all other outside stimulation is avoided. The state is similar to that of someone standing in a spotlight on stage. The hypnotist's suggestions are the focusing beam of the spotlight, and everything else surrounding the subject is dark. By this focusing process, the suggestions that arrive are stronger than they would be if distractions were present. No one can be hypnotized against his or her will, nor once hypnotized can anyone be forced to do something that is strongly against basic personal feelings. However, hypnotism can be dangerous. For example, people still in a hypnotic trance have been hit by autos. Hypnotism is the strongest method of suggestion, but the healing process is helped by every kind of positive suggestion, beginning with the simple reassurance that the sick person can be helped.

KIRLIAN PHOTOGRAPHY

For years, psychics have claimed ability to see a many-colored spiritual aura of light surrounding the human body. The appearance of this halolike effect would depend on the physical and mental state of the person. Today, a photographic process developed in the late 1930s in Russia by an electrician and his wife, the Kirlians, appears to capture on film what the psychics had claimed to see. Neither a camera nor ordinary light is used but instead, electrical energy is supplied by a battery or other power source. A patient's finger, for example, is placed over unexposed film and then given an electrical charge. When the film is developed, the results are sometimes spectacular, the photographs often showing a bright, irregular outline of brilliant colors, called a "corona." The finger itself may be completely dark or may show spots of colored light. (Kirlian photography also uses black and white film.) The result of the photograph depends on the physical and emotional condition of the subject, but it is not affected by perspiration or skin temperature. Photographic technique may play a large role.

Sometimes the finger of a faith healer, when photographed, will show a brilliant corona while that of the sick person to be treated shows merely a dark silhouette. After the faith healer has touched the patient, photographs may show a reversal; the finger of the faith healer is dark and uninteresting looking while the photograph of the patient shows a bright and multicolored corona. It is as if vital energy of the healer has been transferred to the patient. Exactly what these photographs mean is not clearly understood yet, and their importance to medicine has not been determined. However, the great amount of experimental work now being done in this field should give us many answers.

Since the development of Kirlian photography, there is even more interest in psi processes behind the Iron Curtain, especially in the Soviet Union and Czechoslovakia. Very little firsthand information about research in these countries is available, so most reports about the work going on are based on hearsay.

CHAPTER 7

PSI'S OCCULT COUSINS

MEDIUMS AND SPIRITUALISM

Most of the world believes that when a person's physical body dies, the soul or spirit survives. Many people feel that it is possible to get in touch with the ghosts of beloved relatives or friends. The desire in mankind for eternal life makes the concept of life after death very appealing. A century ago persons who claimed special powers to contact the dead, called mediums, became well known and a new religion, spiritualism, was created. Mediums were at the height of their popularity at the end of the last century when the Society for Psychical Research was founded. Today the number of mediums (most are women) has declined because so many of the famous ones were discovered to be frauds.

Mediums are so called because they serve as a go-between, linking the departed spirit and the living person. They are the channels through which spirit communication is made and messages are sent and received.

A fraudulent medium will arrange contact with the "spirit world" in a fairly standard way. She invites a small gathering of believing people who wish to contact someone who is dead. These meetings usually take place in the evening at the home of the medium and are called séances. Typically in a séance the medium will have several people sitting around a table in a circular fashion in a darkened room, holding hands. The medium, at the head of the table, sits quietly for a while, then apparently goes into a trance, during which she seems to be unaware of her surroundings. Suddenly she may say in a strange voice, "Is Uncle John there, is Uncle John there? This is Lydia." Uncle John excitedly tells the medium that he has a niece who died two months ago, and he is overjoyed that he can now communicate with her. The medium then gives a message, presumably in Lydia's voice, which reassures her anxious uncle that she is very happy in the spirit world. The medium's power amazes Uncle John and convinces him that he is indeed in communication with his beloved niece. This procedure continues with the others at the séance. Often, raps on the table and strange musical sounds will be heard, objects may appear to rise mysteriously from the table (levitate), and transparent ghostlike figures can be seen floating across the darkened room. Everyone leaves the séance poorer by many dollars but rewarded beyond mere money by the joy of reunion with a loved one. They usually rush to tell friends about their experience, and the friends in turn make arrangements for a séance. In this way, a flourishing business for a medium is maintained.

What the participants do not know is that the fraudulent medium is most often a combination of good student and magician, who has done her homework well. She knows in advance who is coming and through use of public records, as well as conversations with friends, has learned a great deal about these people and their families. Also the medium can very cleverly work the sound effects and the visual effects (pulling gauze through the air) by using her feet, often aided by another person hiding in the room. She is further helped in her task by the mental state of those attending the séance. These people usually have just lost someone they loved and whom they greatly miss. Their hearts over rule their minds because they want so much to believe they can continue the relationship that was so precious to them.

Harry Houdini, the greatest escape artist of all time and a very fine magician, was the man most responsible for exposing the best-known fraudulent mediums of his day. When Houdini's mother, whom he worshipped, died, he began to consult mediums in a desperate attempt to contact her. Although he wanted to believe, he was too strong and sensible a man to be deceived. During each séance, he became more and more doubtful, having easily seen that tricks were used in every case. When Houdini died, he felt so strongly that spiritualism was a fake that he left with his widow a prize of $25,000 to be paid to the person who could tell her the secret code which he, Houdini, would try to send from the spirit world, a copy of which Mrs. Houdini kept in a safe. No one was ever successful in claiming the reward.

If ESP exists, there are certainly sensitive mediums who are unwittingly getting information from an Uncle John while they believe they are contacting a Lydia. However, they are not likely to use the gimmicks of the fraudulent mediums.

DO-IT-YOURSELF SPIRITUALISM

There are many forms of spiritualism in which no medium is used. In almost all of them, spirits supposedly cause objects to move, a sort of PK power. Most everyone has heard of the power of spirits to affect material objects. The grandfather clock that stops or the dog that howls at the exact moment of death of its owner are familiar stories. Usually, the owner dies hundreds of miles from his home. However, other forms of spiritual PK have become so popular that they are now parlor games. The first of these is the Ouija board. This board is made of polished wood and is marked with the alphabet, numerals, and the words yes and no. The word Ouija (wee-juh) comes from two foreign words each meaning yes, the French *oui* and the German *ja.* Whoever invented it undoubtedly felt that *yes,* the board will answer all your questions. With the Ouija board is a small triangular object called a planchette, which slides over the board to spell out words and answer questions. The planchette is operated by placing your fingers lightly on top of it; then it is supposed to move of its own accord guided by supernatural power. Actually, movement is caused by unconscious muscle movements. (So called automatic writing is based on the same principle. You hold a pencil over a piece of blank paper. Some outside force is supposed to control the pencil but really *you* are responsible for the words which may appear.) In other words, we are actually directing the pointer (or the pencil) by pushing it in the direction we wish. We are answering our own questions and writing our own words. Playing this game, we can learn more about our real feelings. You should try experiments with the Ouija board. You will be able to observe how others use the board and, without knowing it, get the answers they want. This can also be part of your ESP laboratory.

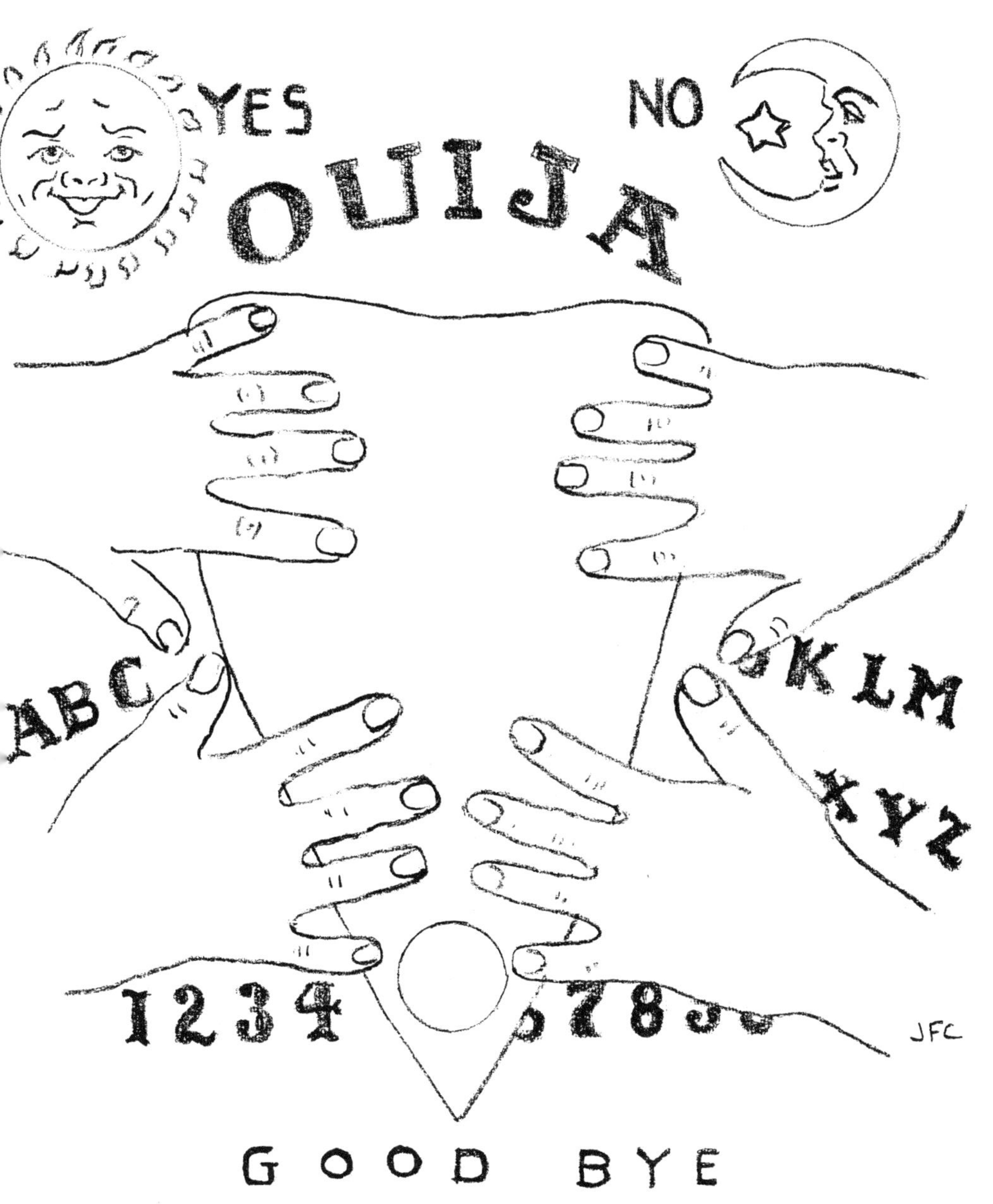
YES
NO
OUIJA
ABC
KLM
XYZ
1234
678
GOOD BYE
JFC

There is another kind of do-it-yourself spiritualism that was very popular in the mid-1800s. Called table turning or table tipping, it was often a social event. A few people would sit around a table with their hands placed lightly on the surface. Each would ask a question and the table would move in some way to give an answer from the supernatural world. Sometimes the table would turn or tip up and down quite violently. Michael Faraday, the great English physicist, investigated table turning and found that people's hands on the table moved first, and the table motion followed. Thus movement, like that of the planchette over the Ouija board, is caused by unconscious movements. Today you can watch demonstrations of table turning on TV as part of a magic act. However, the magicians who perform this kind of trick seldom explain how it works, letting the audience think it is due to supernatural powers.

DÉJÀ VU

Have you ever walked into a room and suddenly had the very strange feeling that you had been in that room sometime before, even though you knew you had never been in the room before? Many people claim that this experience is mystical, due to reincarnation or is the result of earlier out-of-body travels. The experience is called *déjà vu* and comes from two French words meaning "already seen." It is the result of a psychological trick in which many circumstances—lighting, appearance of the room, time of day, state of mind, etc.—are so similar to an event that actually *did* happen that something suddenly "clicks" in your mind and you feel you are repeating an identical experience. Actually, you are repeating an earlier experience so similar that it seems to be identical. Very often you can remember the circumstances of the original event and then can easily understand why you got that funny click in your mind.

POLTERGEISTS

How would you like to be sitting quietly in a room, reading, when suddenly a vase flies off the mantle and crashes against a wall? This kind of frightening experience is reported to happen from time to time and is thought by many to be the work of mischievous ghosts. The word *poltergeists* actually means "noisy ghosts" in German. They have the bad habit of breaking things, making pots and pans rattle and starting mysterious fires. The presence of a young girl or boy is important in order for poltergeist phenomena to occur. The cause of these happenings is unknown.

This type of PK event has never been scientifically shown, but Charles T. Tart has suggested the use of electronic devices to study poltergeists. These methods would detect fraud as well as show the mechanism of any real poltergeist activity. For example, if a person in a supposedly haunted house reports seeing a luminous apparition in a darkened room, Dr. Tart's equipment would detect whether there was something present emitting light or whether the ghost was only in the viewer's mind. In the same way, by installing very sensitive thermometers, his equipment could detect if air in a "haunted" room really became chilly. By using a variety of other electronic aids, such disturbances as noise, vibration and movement of objects could all be detected. It would be fun, although scary, to sit around in a darkened room wired by Dr. Tart, waiting to see which piece of equipment gave the first signal. If everything went off at once, you'd have a very troublesome ghost or ghosts and might need the services of an exorcist.

EXORCISM

During periods of insecurity and fear, many people turn to mystical explanations for their troubles. They seem to need supernatural causes to account for their discomfort. Today there seems to be a revival of interest in the occult, and nowhere is this better demonstrated than in the response to the book and the movie, *The Exorcist,* which has frightened the wits out of millions of people. The story tells of the "possession" of a child by a devil and is based on a true case in which a boy supposedly began to curse in ancient languages and show other strange behavior. After psychiatric care had failed to cure the boy, the ceremony of exorcism was performed. This is a rarely used religious ceremony in which a priest or minister or rabbi uses a special ritual involving a great deal of prayer to "cast out" the devil who has taken possession of the victim's body. Occasionally, demons are exorcized from haunted houses. Many feel that the religious ceremony of exorcism is really another form of psychotherapy in which the victim has more belief in religious than in intellectual power. Most clergy think "possession" is a mental disturbance rather than a supernatural fact, but a small number of clerics continue to believe that demons are responsible for the condition.

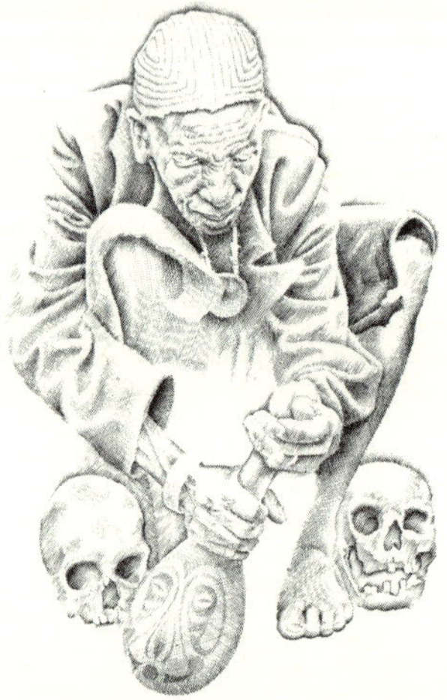

CHAPTER 8

MODERN BRAIN RESEARCH

In the last several years, some very exciting research has been done in the field of brain physiology, a science that deals with brain function. Since nobody denies that if ESP exists, it involves use of the brain in some way, new findings about brain function will have to be incorporated into theories of ESP action. Some findings now considered by ESP investigators to be extrasensory may prove to be sensory and explainable on that basis. For example, bats at one time were thought to be clairvoyant and able to fly in the dark without hitting anything because of this power. Then it was discovered that bats navigated in a *sensory* way, using the echoes of high-pitched sounds they emitted to find their position in a cave. This fact does not disprove the existence of clairvoyance; it simply means that bats are not clairvoyant. Perhaps we possess certain sensory powers not yet discovered. In that case, some of the phenomena we call ESP may actually be EKSP, *extra known sensory perception.*

Cornell University researchers have recently made some discoveries that may explain how birds are able to fly to a distant place never before seen and then to return home safely with uncanny accuracy. These researchers have been the first to find that birds can sense small changes in air pressure equivalent to a drop in altitude of less than twenty feet and also that they can "see" polarized light, which helps them navigate when the sun is obscured by clouds. Migration takes place on relatively few nights of each season at a time when the barometer is falling. Later, a rising barometer is a sign of winds favorable for northward migration in the spring. Information of this sort is undoubtedly integrated by the bird's brain.

Some of the most interesting and fundamental brain research deals with the autonomic nervous system, a part of the nervous system so named because it was supposed to act independently of will, in an involuntary or automatic fashion. Recent research proves that this system has been incorrectly named—to the surprise of all except the imaginative researchers, it can be controlled by conscious thought, using training methods. For example, for years yogis in India and elsewhere were considered to have a great deal of control over breathing processes, and it was felt this was accomplished by some mystical means. A few years ago, researchers in India asked one of the best-known yoga practitioners to volunteer for a laboratory experiment. They placed the yogi in an airtight metal box which had instruments for measuring oxygen and carbon dioxide concentrations. The yogi meditated before he was placed in the box and attached to the instruments, and he continued to meditate during the course of the experiment. To the amazement of the researchers, the yogi was able to remain in the airtight box for several hours because he was able to control the rate at which he burned oxygen. He consumed far less of this vital gas than the scientists had believed possible.

Professor Neal Miller of Rockefeller University in New York City began the studies which showed that higher brain centers could be used to teach control of autonomic functions. The process used is one of biofeedback, a word that means exactly what it says—information about biological processes such as blood pressure state or heart rate is "fed back" to an experimental subject so that he or she can tell what is happening. The feedback is accomplished by visual or auditory instruments; the subject can see on a screen or hear by use of various tones or other sounds the direction of biological change. For example, if a girl is hooked up to a blood pressure machine, which in turn is connected to a sound transmitter, she can learn how to lower or raise her blood pressure, a process thought to be impossible only a few years ago. If she purposely relaxes and the blood pressure begins to drop, a beeping sound tells her that she is relaxing properly to reduce her pressure.

Another important area of brain research involves the processes of learning and memory. How do we handle the enormous amount of sensory information we receive every day? Think of the impressions we get by simply walking down the street. If we are in a city, we will see the sidewalk complete with candy wrappers, pieces of chewing gum, dividing cracks and the like. We will see traffic signals, signs, store windows, garbage cans, automobiles and, of course, people—interesting looking people of all ages, sizes and shapes. We will hear sounds—horns honking, brakes squealing, heels clicking on the pavement. And there will be aromas of all sorts. All of these impressions come from a short walk down the block. No one is certain how much of what we see, hear, taste, touch and smell each day is stored as memories in our brains. Perhaps all of it is, but we are not always able to remember what has been stored. By the word "memory" we usually mean information we can recall or retrieve from the storehouse of our mind. Recently, scientists have been experimenting on some of the factors responsible for long-term memory.

Memory is divided into two types—short-term and long-term. We may learn something quickly, such as a series of words or numbers. However, in order for this information to be transferred to the long-range memory bank, a process called *rehearsal* must take place. Just as actors rehearse their lines for a play by going over them again and again, we form long-term memories by repeatedly reviewing the material we wish to learn. Apparently, rehearsal of material causes the formation of protein in the brain, and this protein is essential for the production of long-term memory.

Finally, interesting experiments have been going on with people whose brains have been split into two halves by a surgical operation. (The surgery is usually done to stop or reduce the number of epileptic attacks). The normal human brain consists of two similar looking halves which are connected so that information can travel from one side to the other and vice versa. In the split-brain person, this transfer of information between the two sides is impossible. People who have had this operation act as if they had two separate brains, and in many tasks they seem to work twice as efficiently, each side of the brain working on a separate task. Certain functions are damaged, however, because

LEFT
RIGHT
POEMS
I can write
I CAN TALK
I CAN SPEAK

the right hand may not know what the left hand is doing. Scientists discovered that the two halves of the brain have different functions. The left half controls verbal functions such as speaking, reading and writing. The right half seems more responsible for visualization of the form of things such as shapes of objects. It also seems to be the "feeling" half, so that appreciation of music and art may come from actions of the right half of the brain. Many psi investigators, aware of this research, feel that the right side of the brain is responsible for ESP.

There is much to learn and many exciting discoveries lie ahead as brain research continues.

CHAPTER 9

WHY THE DOUBT?

Why is there so much argument about ESP today? After all, stories have been told about psychic powers since history was first recorded, and organizations to study these powers have been in existence for almost a hundred years. Scientific experiments with ESP have been taking place for at least three decades. Still, there remains a great deal of doubt about the existence of ESP. There are many reasons for this uncertainty but the most important is simply that in order to prove something is due to ESP, it is necessary to show that no other thing is responsible. This is very hard to do since there are so many possible explanations besides that of ESP. What is needed is a reliable, repeatable experiment which is so controlled that no other explanation, aside from ESP, could explain the results. Most scientists feel that the experiments done so far have not met this test.

ESP investigators say that there would be much more dramatic evidence for ESP in the United States if our culture encouraged it. They also say that those who believe do much better on testing than those who are skeptical. These investigators point out that when we are young children, belief in the mystical is discouraged by parents and other older people, who feel that it is more important for a child to develop "practical" thinking habits.

What are some of the things which have proved difficult for those working in the ESP field? First, there is out-and-out fraud. From its very beginnings, the Society for Psychical Research was injured when honest investigators were fooled repeatedly. Many of the "gifted" subjects were eventually caught cheating or eventually admitted cheating because it was fun to fool the scientists.

The study of ESP has been hampered up to now by a lack of sufficient funds for good research. This is being remedied as more interest in ESP builds, and the result is some of the well-controlled experimental work now being done in the field.

The most difficult problem in ESP research is the fact that possible psi powers are fragile. This means that the atmosphere in which tests are conducted must be congenial and friendly so that the subject being tested feels at ease. The problem is to create a relaxed atmosphere and at the same time make sure that the tests meet scientific standards, a very hard job but certainly not impossible.

No solid proof for the existence of ESP is yet available. The subject is so complex and so exciting that research in the field will continue, and those of you who are interested will have lots of opportunity to make scientific contributions. The serious experimentation which is now beginning should be encouraged.

One final word of caution—those of you who pursue this subject should remain skeptical. Good scientists always question their results, looking for every possible source of error before they reach a conclusion. There is a difference between skepticism and outright hostility. The best investigators in ESP today are the ones who welcome doubt. What is badly needed is cooperative experimentation with skeptics and believers working together and studying subjects who claim to strongly possess special powers. Open-minded scientists must be given an opportunity to rule out fraud or honest mistakes in experimental methods. To date, this has not been done. It deserves to be.

Test Your ESP

Answers appear on page 81.

Cecelia

Nadine

Randi

Alan

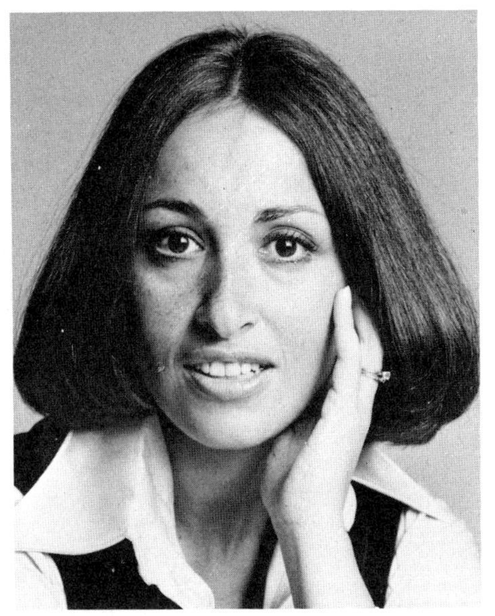

Marcia

Jimmie

ESP investigators claim we can learn a great deal about a person by just looking at his or her picture. Study these six photographs and see if you can answer the following questions about them.

Which two of these people has traveled widely?

Who lives in the same state in which he was born?

Which of these four is musically inclined?

Which of these people has psychic powers?

Which of these two people was born in September?

Can you match the unusual event with the face?

1. At fifteen, signed on board ship as a cabin boy.
2. Spent two hours sealed in an airtight coffin at the bottom of a hotel swimming pool.
3. Wrote a musical comedy in Russian.
4. Walked more than 2500 miles through enemy territory.

How many jobs has she held?

Which of these people have experience raising animals?

What is her favorite color?

Who of these four people was born in a foreign country?

ANSWERS

page 70	*Cecilia*
page 71	*Jimmie*
page 72	*Nadine*
page 73	*Randi*
page 74	*Cecilia*
page 75	*1. Jimmie*
	2. Randi
	3. Alan
	4. Cecilia
page 76	*Twenty-eight*
page 77	*Jimmie*
page 78	*Yellow*
page 79	*Randi & Cecilia*

Glossary

astral projection: The claimed ability to leave one's physical body and travel great distances and then return.

clairvoyance: Knowledge obtained about an object or an event without the use of the senses.

déjà vu: A funny feeling that a new experience has already happened.

ESP (extrasensory perception): The ability to receive mental messages without use of the senses. The four main types of ESP are mental telepathy, clairvoyance, precognition, and psychokinesis or PK.

exorcism: A religious ceremony using prayer to evict a devil who has taken possession of a victim's body.

Kirlian photography: A photographic process which shows an irregular outline (corona) around parts of the body. How the photograph turns out is supposed to depend on the physical and emotional condition of the subject.

medium: A person who serves as a go-between in contacting dead friends and relatives of living persons.

mental telepathy: Thoughts sent by one person and received by another.

parapsychology: The science that deals with the investigation of psychic phenomena.

PK (psychokinesis): Ability to influence physical objects by use of mind power.

poltergeist: A mischievous, noisy ghost who likes to throw things and generally stirs up a fuss.

precognition: A type of clairvoyance in which the person is able to foretell events.

premonition: A sudden feeling which warns a person about something that is going to happen.

psi: Unexplained thought powers.

psychic: A person supposedly gifted with special mental powers.

séance: A meeting of a small group of people conducted by a medium who tries to contact the spirits of dead friends and relatives of those people at the meeting.

spiritualism: A religion which believes that communication is possible between the living and the dead.

Zener cards: A specially designed deck of ESP testing cards.

Index